© 2019 Ryan Morgan
Cover by Ryan Morgan. Images from Vecteezy and Unsplash.

CONTENTS

RESEARCH

PLACES TO GO

PLACES TO EAT

RESEARCH

TRAVEL CALENDAR

MONTH: ....

SUN	MON	TUE	WED	THU	FRI	SAT

Notes:

_____

_____

_____

_____

3

⬠ TRAVEL CALENDAR

MONTH: ....

SUN	MON	TUE	WED	THU	FRI	SAT

Notes:

_____

_____

_____

_____

RESERVATIONS

DESTINATION: ....

Flight:	Confirmation #:
Airport:	Departing:
Airline:	Arriving:

Flight:	Confirmation #:
Airport:	Departing:
Airline:	Arriving:

Rental Car:	Confirmation #:
Rental Company:	
Pick Up:	Drop Off:

Lodging:	Confirmation #:
Check In:	Address:
Check Out:	

Notes:

_____

_____

_____

_____

RESERVATIONS

DESTINATION: ....

Flight:	Confirmation #:
Airport:	Departing:
Airline:	Arriving:

Flight:	Confirmation #:
Airport:	Departing:
Airline:	Arriving:

Rental Car:	Confirmation #:
Rental Company:	
Pick Up:	Drop Off:

Lodging:	Confirmation #:
Check In:	Address:
Check Out:	

Notes:

_____

_____

_____

_____

⚑ TRAVEL BUDGET

EXPENSE	BUDGET	ACTUAL

⚑ TRAVEL BUDGET

EXPENSE	BUDGET	ACTUAL

PACKING LIST

ITEM	☑

⚑ PACKING LIST

ITEM	☑

ITINERARY   DATE: ....

SCHEDULE	
5:00AM	
6:00AM	
7:00AM	
8:00AM	
9:00AM	
10:00AM	
11:00AM	
12:00PM	
1:00PM	
2:00PM	
3:00PM	
4:00PM	
5:00PM	
6:00PM	
7:00PM	
8:00PM	
9:00PM	
10:00PM	
11:00PM	
12:00PM	

MEALS

BREAKFAST:

LUNCH:

DINNER:

ACTIVITIES

NOTES

MEMORIES

DATE: ....

ITINERARY   DATE: ....

SCHEDULE	
5:00AM	
6:00AM	
7:00AM	
8:00AM	
9:00AM	
10:00AM	
11:00AM	
12:00PM	
1:00PM	
2:00PM	
3:00PM	
4:00PM	
5:00PM	
6:00PM	
7:00PM	
8:00PM	
9:00PM	
10:00PM	
11:00PM	
12:00PM	

MEALS

BREAKFAST:

LUNCH:

DINNER:

ACTIVITIES

NOTES

MEMORIES

DATE: ....

ITINERARY

DATE: ....

SCHEDULE	
5:00AM	
6:00AM	
7:00AM	
8:00AM	
9:00AM	
10:00AM	
11:00AM	
12:00PM	
1:00PM	
2:00PM	
3:00PM	
4:00PM	
5:00PM	
6:00PM	
7:00PM	
8:00PM	
9:00PM	
10:00PM	
11:00PM	
12:00PM	

MEALS

BREAKFAST:

LUNCH:

DINNER:

ACTIVITIES

NOTES

MEMORIES

DATE: ....

ITINERARY

DATE: ....

SCHEDULE	
5:00AM	
6:00AM	
7:00AM	
8:00AM	
9:00AM	
10:00AM	
11:00AM	
12:00PM	
1:00PM	
2:00PM	
3:00PM	
4:00PM	
5:00PM	
6:00PM	
7:00PM	
8:00PM	
9:00PM	
10:00PM	
11:00PM	
12:00PM	

MEALS

BREAKFAST:

LUNCH:

DINNER:

ACTIVITIES

NOTES

MEMORIES

DATE: ....

ITINERARY

DATE: ....

SCHEDULE	
5:00 AM	
6:00 AM	
7:00 AM	
8:00 AM	
9:00 AM	
10:00 AM	
11:00 AM	
12:00 PM	
1:00 PM	
2:00 PM	
3:00 PM	
4:00 PM	
5:00 PM	
6:00 PM	
7:00 PM	
8:00 PM	
9:00 PM	
10:00 PM	
11:00 PM	
12:00 PM	

MEALS

BREAKFAST:

LUNCH:

DINNER:

ACTIVITIES

NOTES

MEMORIES

DATE: ....

ITINERARY

DATE: ....

SCHEDULE	
5:00 AM	
6:00 AM	
7:00 AM	
8:00 AM	
9:00 AM	
10:00 AM	
11:00 AM	
12:00 PM	
1:00 PM	
2:00 PM	
3:00 PM	
4:00 PM	
5:00 PM	
6:00 PM	
7:00 PM	
8:00 PM	
9:00 PM	
10:00 PM	
11:00 PM	
12:00 PM	

MEALS

BREAKFAST:

LUNCH:

DINNER:

ACTIVITIES

NOTES

MEMORIES

DATE: ....

ITINERARY

DATE: ....

SCHEDULE	
5:00 AM	
6:00 AM	
7:00 AM	
8:00 AM	
9:00 AM	
10:00 AM	
11:00 AM	
12:00 PM	
1:00 PM	
2:00 PM	
3:00 PM	
4:00 PM	
5:00 PM	
6:00 PM	
7:00 PM	
8:00 PM	
9:00 PM	
10:00 PM	
11:00 PM	
12:00 PM	

MEALS

BREAKFAST:

LUNCH:

DINNER:

ACTIVITIES

NOTES

MEMORIES

DATE: ....

ITINERARY

DATE: ....

SCHEDULE	
5:00 AM	
6:00 AM	
7:00 AM	
8:00 AM	
9:00 AM	
10:00 AM	
11:00 AM	
12:00 PM	
1:00 PM	
2:00 PM	
3:00 PM	
4:00 PM	
5:00 PM	
6:00 PM	
7:00 PM	
8:00 PM	
9:00 PM	
10:00 PM	
11:00 PM	
12:00 PM	

MEALS

BREAKFAST:

LUNCH:

DINNER:

ACTIVITIES

NOTES

MEMORIES

DATE: ....

ITINERARY

DATE: ....

SCHEDULE	
5:00 AM	
6:00 AM	
7:00 AM	
8:00 AM	
9:00 AM	
10:00 AM	
11:00 AM	
12:00 PM	
1:00 PM	
2:00 PM	
3:00 PM	
4:00 PM	
5:00 PM	
6:00 PM	
7:00 PM	
8:00 PM	
9:00 PM	
10:00 PM	
11:00 PM	
12:00 PM	

MEALS

BREAKFAST:

LUNCH:

DINNER:

ACTIVITIES

NOTES

MEMORIES

ITINERARY

DATE: ....

SCHEDULE	
5:00 AM	
6:00 AM	
7:00 AM	
8:00 AM	
9:00 AM	
10:00 AM	
11:00 AM	
12:00 PM	
1:00 PM	
2:00 PM	
3:00 PM	
4:00 PM	
5:00 PM	
6:00 PM	
7:00 PM	
8:00 PM	
9:00 PM	
10:00 PM	
11:00 PM	
12:00 PM	

MEALS

BREAKFAST:

LUNCH:

DINNER:

ACTIVITIES

NOTES

MEMORIES

DATE: ....

ITINERARY DATE: ....

SCHEDULE	
5:00 AM	
6:00 AM	
7:00 AM	
8:00 AM	
9:00 AM	
10:00 AM	
11:00 AM	
12:00 PM	
1:00 PM	
2:00 PM	
3:00 PM	
4:00 PM	
5:00 PM	
6:00 PM	
7:00 PM	
8:00 PM	
9:00 PM	
10:00 PM	
11:00 PM	
12:00 PM	

MEALS

BREAKFAST:

LUNCH:

DINNER:

ACTIVITIES

NOTES

MEMORIES

DATE: ....

ITINERARY

DATE: ....

SCHEDULE	
5:00 AM	
6:00 AM	
7:00 AM	
8:00 AM	
9:00 AM	
10:00 AM	
11:00 AM	
12:00 PM	
1:00 PM	
2:00 PM	
3:00 PM	
4:00 PM	
5:00 PM	
6:00 PM	
7:00 PM	
8:00 PM	
9:00 PM	
10:00 PM	
11:00 PM	
12:00 PM	

MEALS

BREAKFAST:

LUNCH:

DINNER:

ACTIVITIES

NOTES

MEMORIES

DATE: ....

ITINERARY

DATE: ....

SCHEDULE	
5:00AM	
6:00AM	
7:00AM	
8:00AM	
9:00AM	
10:00AM	
11:00AM	
12:00PM	
1:00PM	
2:00PM	
3:00PM	
4:00PM	
5:00PM	
6:00PM	
7:00PM	
8:00PM	
9:00PM	
10:00PM	
11:00PM	
12:00PM	

MEALS

BREAKFAST:

LUNCH:

DINNER:

ACTIVITIES

NOTES

MEMORIES

DATE: ....

ITINERARY DATE: ....

SCHEDULE	
5:00AM	
6:00AM	
7:00AM	
8:00AM	
9:00AM	
10:00AM	
11:00AM	
12:00PM	
1:00PM	
2:00PM	
3:00PM	
4:00PM	
5:00PM	
6:00PM	
7:00PM	
8:00PM	
9:00PM	
10:00PM	
11:00PM	
12:00PM	

MEALS

BREAKFAST:

LUNCH:

DINNER:

ACTIVITIES

NOTES

MEMORIES

DATE: ....

TRAVEL NOTES

TRAVEL NOTES

TRAVEL NOTES

TRAVEL NOTES

TRAVEL NOTES

TRAVEL NOTES

TRAVEL NOTES

TRAVEL NOTES

TRAVEL NOTES

TRAVEL NOTES

TRAVEL NOTES

TRAVEL NOTES

TRAVEL NOTES

TRAVEL NOTES

TRAVEL NOTES

TRAVEL NOTES

TRAVEL NOTES

TRAVEL NOTES

TRAVEL NOTES

TRAVEL NOTES

TRAVEL NOTES

Made in the USA
Middletown, DE
04 March 2023

26152953R00036